About Virtues and Vices

Les Miller

NOVALIS

© 2012 Novalis Publishing Inc.

Cover design: Mardigrafe
Cover illustration: Anna Payne-Krzyzanowski
Interior images: pp. 8, 23, 29, 40: Jupiter Images; pp. 11, 15, 16: Plaisted;
p. 13 (both images): W.P. Wittman; pp. 25, 38: Crestock
Layout: Mardigrafe and Audrey Wells

Published by Novalis

Publishing Office
10 Lower Spadina Avenue, Suite 400
Toronto, Ontario, Canada
M5V 2Z2

Head Office
4475 Frontenac Street
Montréal, Québec, Canada
H2H 2S2

www.novalis.ca

Library and Archives Canada Cataloguing in Publication

Miller, Les, 1952-
      25 questions about virtues and vices / Les Miller.

ISBN 978-2-89646-398-5

1. Theological virtues--Juvenile literature. 2. Cardinal
virtues--Juvenile literature. 3. Deadly sins--Juvenile
literature. I. Title. II. Title: Twenty-five questions about
virtues and vices.

BV4630.M55   2012 j241'.4   C2012-900809-5

Printed in Canada.

We acknowledge the financial support of the Government of Canada through
the Canada Book Fund for business development activities.

5 4 3 2 1   16 15 14 13 12

A word from the author

For ten years, I was involved in the Character Education program in schools in York Region, just north of Toronto. During this time I worked with teachers, administrators and community leaders to help develop resources for students on this topic. Our team created prayers, posters and classroom activities and shared these with the schools.

Why did we create these resources? We wanted to help students develop their virtues. In this book, you will read that virtues are your God-given gifts that help build and strengthen your relationship with God, your community, your friends and your family. Your virtues also help you to be a happier person. In this book, you will explore the three theological virtues and the four cardinal virtues.

Some actions can lead you away from living a good life. These are called vices. In this book we focus on the seven deadly sins. These are bad habits that stop you from being as happy as you could be. They also harm your relationship with God and with other people. To avoid having vices, the key is to develop your virtues. Looking at vices gives us another opportunity to talk about these good habits we all need to encourage in ourselves and others.

I would like to dedicate this book to the Character Community Foundation of York Region and the students of York Catholic District School Board, who helped me to develop many of these ideas.

Les Miller

What is a virtue?

For the third time in one evening, your younger sister asks you for help with her math homework. You stop your own work on an assignment to explain a concept. Sound familiar? Then you are a person of **virtue**! Taking time to help someone is an example of practising the virtues of kindness and patience. A virtue is an action that reflects God, helps others, and helps you, too.

There are dozens of virtues. We'll explore some of them in this book. The seven major virtues we will look at lead to other virtues, such as joy, truth, compassion, harmony, forgiveness, respect, responsibility, honesty and peace.

In our relationships, we have choices about how to treat one another. In the example I gave above, you could have ignored your sister's request for homework help or even told her off for disturbing you. Instead, you chose the path of virtue because you love and respect your sister and want what is best for her.

Why are we virtuous? At one level, we have been taught that it is our duty to be virtuous. God has given us laws, such as the Ten Commandments, to protect and nourish virtue. The Church guides us, too, using the Bible and the ongoing **wisdom** and teaching of the Holy Spirit to let us know our duty when it comes to the virtues.

But it's more than following rules. At another level, we all have a vision of the kind of person we want to become. Most of us want to be loved and respected. For this to happen, we need to be loving and respectful people. Living a virtuous life helps us to be the type of person we want to be.

When we meet people who need our help, we usually do our part. This might mean doing chores at home, taking care of a younger sibling, or carrying groceries for an elderly neighbour. It might not be convenient or fun, but we do it anyway. When people are in need and we respond, we are practising virtue. This practice becomes a **habit** or pattern of goodness. We practise virtue because we care for other people.

 The word "virtue" is from the Greek word *arete*, which also means "excellence."

What is a vice?

Vices are the opposite of virtues. They are patterns or habits of making bad choices that hurt our friendship with God and others. Vices may make us feel uncomfortable with the type of person we have become.

Vices are rooted in selfishness. That means we put our own needs first, rather than thinking about the needs of others or about what God asks us to do. Vices are called **sins** because they hurt our relationship with God. (More on this point in question 16.) God does not love you any less when you allow vices to control your life. But you may feel far from God if you replace your love for God with other desires.

Vices can become habits. For example, someone may start swearing to be accepted by a group of friends. Over time, bad language becomes a habit. Swearing is a vice because it uses God's name disrespectfully or uses harsh words to hurt others.

 Blasphemy is speaking out against God or using God's name as a swear word. The second commandment tells us we should not take God's name in vain (Exodus 20:7). Instead, we should always speak God's name with love and respect.

What do the Ten Commandments tell us about virtues and vices?

We live in a complicated world. It is sometimes hard to tell right from wrong. But that's nothing new! The people of ancient Israel had the same problem. God loved them in a special way and gave them a set of rules for living. The most important of these were the Ten Commandments (found in chapter 20 of the Book of Exodus):

1. You shall have no other gods before me.
2. You shall not make wrongful use of the name of the Lord your God.
3. Remember the **sabbath** day, and keep it holy.
4. Honour your father and your mother.
5. You shall not murder.

6. You shall not commit **adultery**.
7. You shall not steal.
8. You shall not bear **false witness** against your neighbour.
9. You shall not **covet** your neighbour's wife.
10. You shall not covet your neighbour's goods.

(The terms in **bold** type are explained in the Words to Know section at the end of the book.)

You can see that these are very specific rules that tell us what we should do and what we should avoid doing. When we obey these rules again and again, they become habits. We don't

MOSES RECEIVES THE TEN COMMANDMENTS ON TWO STONE TABLETS.

have to think about stealing to know that is wrong. It becomes a habit to respect other people's property. Our **conscience**, which is the part of us that guides our actions to do what is right, helps us here. Our conscience is where God's love meets our ability to make decisions. When we ignore our conscience, we feel troubled and uneasy. When this happens, we must look back on our decisions to find out what we can do so we can feel right with God again.

God gave Moses and the people of Israel the Ten Commandments after leading them out of Egypt, where they had been slaves. The Ten Commandments are also known as the Decalogue, which means "ten words."

?????????? **4** ??????????

What do the biblical prophets teach us about virtues and vices?

After the Israelites settled in the Promised Land, they often forgot about the Ten Commandments and God's other hopes for them. They were tempted by the vices practised by the other people they met. Sometimes they worshipped false gods, straying from the love of God who had led them out of slavery in Egypt. We do the same thing at times. We act as though other things are more important than our relationship with God. If we care more about sports or fashion than about loving God, then we are like the Israelites when they worshipped false gods.

When it seemed as if the Israelites had forgotten all about God, God sent prophets to get them back on track. Prophets, who are God's messengers, reminded the people of the virtues God wanted them to live. In the desert, God had taught them about community. Good families and communities need the virtues of compassion, kindness, wisdom and justice to be successful. Even though the Jewish people were tempted by other voices, and often ignored the prophets, the call to return to God's laws of virtue came again and again.

Today, it is sometimes hard to hear the call to live a life of virtue because of other voices, such as the media, telling us to care only for ourselves or our possessions. But if we listen, we can still hear prophetic voices calling us to live a life of virtue.

 Prophetic voices of recent times include Blessed Mother Teresa, who reminded us of the virtue of caring for the poor, and Blessed Pope John Paul II, who placed so much trust in young people. Can you think of any other modern prophets? Who is a prophet in your own life?

BLESSED MOTHER TERESA OF CALCUTTA

BLESSED JOHN PAUL II

What does Jesus teach us about virtues?

Jesus followed in the footsteps of the wise teachers of the Old Testament in teaching about virtue. For example, he taught people the virtue of following God's laws. He also stressed that living a good life was more than following rules. As well as following the Ten Commandments, we must *want* to live lives of virtue and goodness. Jesus taught us about these attitudes in the Sermon on the Mount, or the Beatitudes. (Some people call them "be-attitudes," because they teach us how to be loving people.) Jesus says that caring, gentleness, peace and justice are important virtues. Not only should we treasure them, but we should put them into practice. As Jesus showed us, you can't just be a person who values peace – you have to be a peacemaker in your everyday life.

Jesus taught the virtue of forgiveness as a practical way of making peace. Conflicts grow when people hit back at each other. Misunderstandings become arguments and then can turn into fights. Jesus taught us to stop this buildup of anger. By looking at the conflict from the other person's point of view, we can begin to forgive one another. Jesus gave us the **Golden Rule** to guide us: "In everything do to others as you would have them do to you." (Matthew 7:12)

Through stories called **parables**, Jesus taught about many other virtues. (You can read more about parables in *25 Questions about the Bible*.) The life of Jesus is our greatest example of a life of virtue. He showed us the power of love with his willingness to die for us. He stood up to injustice even though it cost him his life. He couldn't stop being kind, even to the soldiers who crucified him.

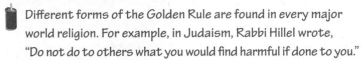

Different forms of the Golden Rule are found in every major world religion. For example, in Judaism, Rabbi Hillel wrote, "Do not do to others what you would find harmful if done to you."

What does the Church teach us about virtues?

In the history of the Catholic Church, brave men and women have shown us that it is possible to live lives of virtue even in tough situations. One of the ways the Church recognizes a person as a saint is through his or her life of virtue. It has to be obvious that a person has shown "heroic virtue" if he or she is to be recognized as a saint.

St. Paul showed the virtue of **dedication** in spreading the Christian message to Greek-speaking communities 2,000 years ago. Even though he was imprisoned, driven out of town, rejected by his friends and often misunderstood, Paul kept on teaching people about Jesus and the God of love.

St. Thomas Aquinas was a priest who taught students

ST. THOMAS AQUINAS (1225–1274)

in the University of Paris about 750 years ago. He was known for his great **wisdom**. He was able to bring together the Christian message with other types of thinking to show how God is at work in the world.

St. Maximilian Kolbe was a Polish Catholic priest who was put in a death camp called Auschwitz by the Nazis during the Second World War. In these camps, people were killed only because they were Jewish or belonged to other groups the Nazis hated. Fr. Maximilian volunteered to take the place of a Jewish person who had been selected to die. He showed the virtue of **courage** in facing death.

 Read about some amazing Catholics in *25 Questions About Catholic Saints and Heroes* or on the Internet. Which virtues does each one show?

What are the theological virtues?

The **theological virtues** are faith, hope and love. Theology is our study of God or those things that come from God. St. Anselm said that theology was "faith seeking understanding." A virtue is theological if it clearly comes from God. Faith, hope and love are all seen as special gifts of God.

St. Paul speaks of the importance of these three virtues in his letter to the people of Corinth. At the end of a beautiful passage, he names the virtues of faith, hope and love, but concludes that love is the greatest of the three. (1 Corinthians 13:13) This reading is often used at weddings.

Faith, hope and love are special gifts because we can't get them through our own efforts. God offers us all these gifts freely. When we trust in God, we accept the faith God gives us. When we hope, we look to the future knowing God will take care of us, even when things are difficult. We love because God loved us first, even before we were born. God shows his love for us by guiding us and being with us through this life and into heaven.

- The word "theology" comes from two Greek words: *theos* (God) and *logia* (sayings).

Sometimes the theological virtues are shown as symbols:
- cross (faith)
- anchor (hope)
- heart (love)

8

What is faith?

Faith is our way of knowing and loving God. We can't know God by using our eyes or ears, but we know God exists and loves us. Faith is God's way of letting us know God is with us. Faith is a theological or God-given virtue. When we were created, we were given the ability to know God. As we grow, we learn more about God from our family, our church community and (for some students) our school.

Knowing God is different from *knowing about* God. We know about God by finding out information from the Bible and from Church teachings. Knowing God directly involves prayer. We speak to God in prayer, but we also try to be open to God's presence in prayer.

Faith is also about how we love God. Remember that love is a gift God gives us that allows us to connect with other people. We respond to this gift by having faith in God.

Some people seem to lose their faith in God. They trust in other ways of looking at life. For example, some believe that science explains everything and so there is no need for faith. Catholic scientists as well as recent Church leaders have responded that science answers questions about how nature works, but science cannot give us answers to our deepest questions: Why is there anything at all in the universe? Why is there love? Why is there beauty? Why do we value truth? We find answers to these questions through faith.

 A person who does not believe in God is called an atheist. Someone who believes that nothing can be known about the existence or nature of God is called an agnostic.

? ? ? ? ? ? ? ? ? ? ? **9** ? ? ? ? ? ? ? ?

How can we become more hopeful people?

Hope is looking to the future knowing that we will be okay. It is the virtue that Jesus modelled, especially in the days before he died on the cross. He knew he was facing death, but he continued to teach and heal people, giving them gifts that would help them spread his message in the years to come.

Jesus could easily have given in to despair. Most of his followers and friends had abandoned him. He was to suffer the shame of a criminal's death. He knew that crucifixion would be an extremely painful death. Yet Jesus was full of hope. The event that gives us Christians the greatest hope is the resurrection, when God raised Jesus from the dead. It shows us that even death is not the end.

When we are faced with problems, hope can help us. When we look to the future with faith and love, we know God is with us. We know that even though we hurt and will eventually die, God will never stop loving us and guiding us.

When we are hopeful, we know that difficulties and challenges are not bad things. Hope can help us to make the best of tough situations. Remember that love is a virtue that links us to God and to other people. When we hope, we connect to a future where love can guide our lives.

Hope is not an unrealistic wish for only good things to happen. Life will present us with hard times. God's gift of hope helps us to meet these challenges and even grow from them.

 Hope is celebrated in a special way at Advent. At the beginning of the Church year, we look forward in hope to the celebration of Christ's birth at Christmas. For this reason, the first candle on the Advent wreath is sometimes called the "Hope Candle."

Is love more than a feeling?

Love lies at the heart of our humanity. It is much more than a strong feeling for another person. Although we often say we "love" something – like a singer, a movie, or even a certain kind of food, this isn't real love. Love is about relationship, about choosing to be with someone through thick and thin. Love is a powerful gift from God. This power comes from love's ability to bring people together. Love makes people want to know each other. We find this love in family and friendships, where love grows and is shared with more and more people. Love brings couples together to marry and create families. In fact, all creation is filled with God's love.

Love is so powerful, it can help us to mend differences between people. Do you remember your first day in a new class or club or on a new team? You may have felt alone or unsure of yourself. You may not have known anyone. Over time, you made friends and felt more at home. Even if you had problems with your new friends, you would have wanted to heal the hurt. This is God's gift of love in action in your life.

Our ability to love is the greatest gift we have. God has given us this gift to make our lives and this world better – to help those who are hurting because of poverty, disease or war, and to help the environment, too.

 St. Paul wrote in the ancient Greek language. His word for this kind of love was *agape* [ah-gah-pay]. It is sometimes translated into English as "charity." **Charity** in this sense means giving the gift of love to others through offering support, sharing friendship or doing acts of justice.

What are the cardinal virtues?

The traditional words for the four **cardinal virtues** are prudence, justice, temperance and fortitude. They are called *cardinal* virtues because they are named for the Latin word for hinge (*cardo*). A door needs hinges to work. In the same way, our relationships depend on the cardinal virtues to work well.

What are some more modern terms for these virtues? Prudence means wisdom for living. Justice is treating people fairly. Temperance is using self-control when we make choices. Fortitude means courage. We'll look at each one of these in the next few questions.

For centuries, the cardinal virtues and the theological virtues gave guidance to people who were trying to live a good life. Rather than acting on emotions and feelings, people lived these virtues to prevent problems and to heal wounds caused by conflicts. People learned these virtues from their churches, families and friends. In recent centuries, these virtues have also been taught in schools.

 Cardinal virtues are *not* named after the Church leaders who gather to elect a pope.

How can I become a wiser person?

Some situations make us feel angry, afraid, calm or happy. These are feelings. Feelings are neither good nor bad. They are simply our human response to what happens to us. How we act on our feelings is up to us. The more we can act with virtue in response to our feelings, the better our lives will be.

Let's say you are angry because a friend has called you a bad name. Your instincts tell you to hurl an insult back. But wait a minute. The wisest thing to do is take some time to understand why your friend is upset. Knowing the reason behind a friend's bad behaviour can help stop an ugly fight and can help your friend deal with things better. Prudence or wisdom tells you that you have a choice in a conflict – to harm or to heal.

The wise thing to do includes

- Pausing and not reacting right away;
- Listening for the reasons for the anger;
- Asking polite questions to understand the reasons for the conflict;
- Bringing God into the situation. In this form of prayer, you imagine how Jesus or another holy person would act if they were in your shoes.

St. Augustine and St. Thomas Aquinas both saw prudence as the way we wisely bring Christian love into our lives.

??????????? **13** ????????

What's the difference between justice and equality?

Justice involves making sure people have what is owed to them. For example, if you borrow something from a friend, it is only just that you return it to them later. In a global sense, justice calls people to share the gifts of clean water and other basic needs. People who have these gifts should work to help others get them, too. One way of living justly is to find out where and why people don't have the basic necessities for living, such as food, water, education, safety and shelter. Then you can look for ways to change things for the better.

In the Bible, we see that the prophets and Jesus often taught about justice. Jesus said he is present in those people who lack the basic needs of life. (See the Gospel of Matthew, chapter 25.) We should always treat everyone as if they were Christ himself.

One system of justice is equality. This means treating everyone fairly, so all have the same rights, no matter what their race or ethnic background is, or whether they are male or female. Justice tells us that everybody deserves a fair chance to succeed in a group.

When we practise justice, we bring wisdom and love to situations so that all can succeed.

 Laws in North America are mostly based on Jewish and Christian ideas of justice. But justice as a virtue is about more than following laws. We are just when we see and act on problems that stop people from living good and happy lives.

Why is self-control important?

The virtue of self-control used to be known as temperance. A Greek thinker called Aristotle [Air-iss-stot-el] asked, "What makes us happy?" His answer was balance, or the **golden mean**. For example, we desire food because we need it to survive, but it also gives us pleasure. If we don't eat enough, we can starve. If we eat too much, our bodies can become unhealthy. Aristotle thought we ought to find a happy medium and show self-control when we eat.

Another kind of self-control is in how we choose our friends. Sometimes we want to be friends with people even though they do things we know are wrong, like swearing, stealing or trying cigarettes or drugs. Or maybe we only want friends who have the same interests, because we don't want to try new things. Aristotle said finding a balance between the two extremes will make for happier friendships.

 A hundred years ago, "temperance" became a political word in North America. The Temperance movement aimed to outlaw the drinking of alcohol, because alcohol abuse had harmful effects on families and others.

What is true courage?

We see many dramatic examples of **courage** in the news, in movies and in sports. Often these acts involve taking risks in dramatic situations. But courage is a virtue you can practise daily in smaller but very important ways.

The virtue of courage was once called "fortitude," which comes from a word that means "strength." We need moral strength to do what we know is right. Courage comes into play when it joins with other virtues.

- It takes courage to be faithful in a world where some people don't believe in God.

- It takes courage to be hopeful when despair and cynicism seem to be cool.

- It takes courage to love when there is so much hatred and fear around us.

- It takes courage to be wise when it is easier to react without thinking things through.

- It takes courage to be just and to stand up for those who don't have the basic things they need to survive.

- It takes courage to have self-control when so many celebrities seem to do whatever they want.

The everyday courage we need to live a life of virtue makes us heroes.

 A common saying in the Bible is "Don't be afraid" or "Take heart." Jesus asks us to stand up for what we know is good and true: in other words, to have the courage to live lives of virtue.

What is sin?

We first hear about sin in the Bible when we read the story of Adam and Eve. (See Genesis, chapters 2 and 3.) They disobeyed God and ate from the tree of the knowledge of good and evil. Later, knowing they had done wrong, they tried to hide from God. This story shows two ways of looking at sin: breaking God's rules and hiding from God. The result is broken relationships with God, with other people, and even with ourselves.

As Catholics, we are asked to follow the rules God has set for us in the Bible. The Church also guides us in how to live. These rules are not meant to limit our freedom, but to show us how to live good and loving lives. We sin when we decide not to follow these ways of living.

You can try to hide from God by refusing to pray, not going to Mass or forgetting about God entirely. You can follow other people instead of following God. You can let other activities become more important than being with God. But even if you try to separate yourself from God's love, you cannot stop God from loving you. God always welcomes you back through the Sacrament of Reconciliation, where you tell the priest what you have done and he gives you **absolution** in the name of the Father, and of the Son, and of the Holy Spirit. Now your sins are forgiven and you can have a fresh start. (See *25 Questions about the Sacraments* for more on Reconciliation.)

 The sin of Adam and Eve is called "original sin." At Baptism, Jesus washes away our sin and we are welcomed into God's family, the Church.

?????????? **17** ??????????

What are the seven deadly sins, and why are they *deadly?*

The seven deadly sins are pride, envy, lust, anger, gluttony, greed and sloth. (If some of these words are new to you, don't worry. I will explain them in the next few questions.)

They are called *deadly* sins because they can lead to a kind of spiritual death where we stop being aware of God. They are powerful because they can lead to other sins. For example, if you are overly proud, you can ignore the needs of others. If you envy your friend's clothes, you might steal money to buy similar clothes for yourself.

The Church developed the list of the seven deadly sins to help people understand how sin can harm their lives. The seven deadly sins match the number of the theological virtues (three) plus the cardinal virtues (four).

 The seven deadly sins are sometimes called the seven "capital" sins. "Capital" comes from the Latin word *caput*, which means "head." The head controls the body. The capital or deadly sins control other sins.

18

What's wrong with pride?

We are often told to be proud of who we are or to take pride in our school or community. Used in this way, pride seems to be more of a virtue than a vice. With this kind of pride, we celebrate our gifts, our human dignity, and the fact that God is at work in our lives. But the Church lists pride as the first of the deadly sins. Why?

Pride can easily turn into arrogance and selfishness. As soon as we disconnect our personal achievements from God's work in us, we begin to think we can do everything ourselves. We think we don't need anyone else, or even God. We become arrogant when we think we are better than other people. We might even start to show them we think we are superior.

Excess pride also leads to selfishness. We think and act as if our needs are more important than other people's. We stop caring what others think, and do whatever suits us. Selfishness blinds us from reaching out to others and stops virtues from thriving. In a way, selfishness is the opposite of love. Love causes us to reach out to others. Selfishness turns us inward and away from others in our search for happiness. Selfish and arrogant pride can be seen as the root of other sins.

 The Bible criticizes people who are full of pride. In the book of Genesis (chapter 11), we read about the pride of the people of Babel. They wanted to be like God, so they tried to build a tower to heaven. God mixed up their language so they couldn't understand each other, and the people were scattered over the whole earth.

How can I stop being jealous?

When you are jealous or envious, you want things that someone else has. You might be jealous of a friend's new phone, or abilities, or looks, or even their whole life! Notice that selfishness is at work here. When you get caught up in your own desires, you can't be happy about the good things a friend has going for them. You are thinking only of yourself.

What you do with your feelings of envy is the important thing. If you allow envy to become a habit, you will keep feeling that other people have better things than you. This is a negative view of the world and will make you unhappy. Envy can hurt your relationship with your brothers and sisters, your classmates and your friends.

If you think envy is a problem for you, talk to your parents or another trusted adult. Or talk to a priest in the Sacrament of Reconciliation. They will encourage you to see all the positive things in your life and to be thankful for them. God is generous!

 Jealousy is sometimes called "the green-eyed monster." People are described as being "green with envy."

Why is lust wrong?

Lust is a strong desire for something. It is a vice because it is selfish and it harms our relationship with others and God. If you lust after someone, you are seeing them as an object to get, not as a beloved son or daughter of God. You are trying to please yourself, not God.

Chastity means having respect for yourself, the other person and God. After all, each person is created by God to live a life of love for others. By focusing on healthy relationships and healthy activities, you can avoid lust.

Sexual feelings are gifts from God that draw couples together in love and create new life. The place to express these feelings fully is in marriage. Chastity helps us to balance our sexual feelings and stay in control of them until we are married.

 Chastity is not the same thing as celibacy. Chastity is using our sexual gifts responsibly. **Celibacy** is choosing not to marry or have sexual relationships. Priests, religious sisters and brothers take a vow of celibacy.

How can I deal with my anger?

Anger is both a feeling and a vice. We have no control over what we feel, but we do have control over how we act on our feelings. You may feel angry that someone is bullying your friend, but it is wrong to express your anger by punching the bully. If you have a pattern of expressing your anger using hurtful words, physical violence or other negative actions, then anger has become a vice.

Anger can be used for good if you deal with it constructively. For example, you can organize with friends and teachers to stop the bullying. Anger can give you energy to work against other forms of injustice, too. If you are angry at the way the earth is being mistreated, you can learn more about environmental issues and find ways of reducing waste, protecting plants and animals at risk of extinction, and saving energy.

Dealing with anger in the heat of the moment isn't easy. When we are angry, chemicals in our brain get us ready to react in a physical way. After a few seconds, these chemicals begin to decrease. The trick is to wait a bit before you respond. (You may have been told to count to ten when you are provoked.) Before you tell the other person why you are angry, make sure both of you are calm. If the feelings are strong, say, "Let's cool off and talk about it later."

St. Paul knew that anger can be both positive and negative. He wrote to the people of Ephesus (Eh-fah-suss), "Be angry, but do not sin." (Ephesians 4:26)

22

Why is gluttony harmful?

*G*luttony is the habit of eating and drinking more than we need. It is harmful because it makes us selfish. Instead of sharing food with the hungry, we eat it ourselves. Instead of respecting the body God has given us, we don't take care of it. Instead of thinking of others, we care only about satisfying our own wishes.

Eating is a good example of finding balance. Eating and drinking give us nutrition and pleasure. If we eat too little, we starve or are malnourished. If we eat and drink too much, we become gluttons.

Gluttony is an issue of justice. In a world where millions of people don't have enough to eat, it is wrong for other people to overeat.

 "Gluttony" comes from the Latin word *gluttire*, meaning to swallow or gulp down.

What's wrong with being greedy?

Greed is called "coveting" in the Ten Commandments. It is a strong desire to have what others have. In the tenth commandment, God tells us directly not to covet what others have. Still, it is hard to avoid greed in our society. We are bombarded with ads that encourage us to want things we don't have (and usually don't need). Greed is a common vice, and a dangerous one.

Greed is a "deadly" sin because it leads to other sins. If people are greedy, they may lie, cheat or steal to get what they want. They are willing to take shortcuts to get things.

They spend so much time thinking and plotting about what they desire, they forget to think about other people's needs.

Greed can become addictive. Have you ever wanted a videogame badly? You are so happy when you first get it, and then within a week or two you are bored and want a new game. Our lives can become cluttered with so many things. We see what our friends have and we want the same or better. If we don't have the latest fashion or gadget, we feel there is something wrong with us.

The Bible and the Church warn us that spending so much time and energy on getting and having things we don't need can lead us away from God. In a way, we are saying we don't have enough time for God. A way to deal with greed is to practise the virtue of generosity. Each day we can ask ourselves this question: What can I give away to others to make their lives better? Your gift may be something to wear, or play with, or read, but a gift of your friendship and time is even better. Make it a habit to make someone else's day with your kindness.

 Another word for this sin is **avarice**. It means wanting other people's things or keeping our own things to ourselves so others can't use them.

So I'm messy. What's the big deal?

"**S loth**" is the traditional word for messiness. We are slothful when laziness stops us from taking care of our appearance and our space, such as our bedroom. It can also mean we don't use our time wisely. We show little care or enthusiasm for others or for our surroundings.

Not caring about ourselves or our living conditions is a sign of disrespect. We are showing that we don't think God's gift of life for us is worth very much. (If we take things to the opposite extreme and care too much about how we look, this is the sin of vanity. It's not a "deadly" sin, but it's still better to avoid it!)

A messy bedroom is also a sign of disrespect to other people. It sends the message that we don't care about our home or the feelings of the people we share it with. If we depend on others to keep things neat and tidy for us, we are saying that our time is more important than theirs. That's not fair to them.

By keeping our things in order and keeping ourselves neat and clean, we let others know we are good stewards of God's gifts.

 Some writers have said that the opposite of sloth is joy. If we are joyful, we will want to make our surroundings as positive as possible.

What does virtue have to do with character?

*C*atholics believe that virtues – especially the theological virtues of faith, hope and love – are gifts from God. **Character** is all the qualities – positive or negative – that make up a person. Our true character tends to shine through our relationships. Our actions show who we really are. Do we put others first? Or is it always about us? By working to develop positive virtues, we can build strong character.

Our character changes and grows as we get older. **Psychologists** tell us it is natural for infants to be self-centred. They are helpless and depend on others to care for them. As we mature, we become better at having concern and care for others. Think about your character strengths. How did you get there? Now look at areas that need work. Where do you go from here? Ask a trusted adult for guidance and feedback if you need it. And be sure to ask God to help you to develop your gifts and share them with others. After all, that's what they're for!

Many Catholic and public schools in North America offer character education programs that encourage young people to grow in virtue and treat one another better. Many of these schools highlight a character attribute or virtue every month, including many of the virtues explored in this book. Catholic character education helps to build on God's work and to celebrate these virtues. Try picking one virtue a month that you would like to develop. Write down how it feels as you go along.

Absolution: part of the Sacrament of Reconciliation where the priest forgives someone in God's name.

Adultery: a sexual relationship between someone who is married and someone who is not their husband or wife.

Avarice: the strong desire to want goods, money and power and not share them with anyone else.

Blasphemy: speaking out against God or using God's name as a swear word.

Cardinal virtues: prudence, justice, temperance and fortitude.

Character: the qualities a person develops.

Charity: self-giving love that is concerned about the well-being of other people.

Chastity: the responsible use of God's gift of sexuality.

Conscience: our inner sense of knowing what is right and what is wrong.

Courage: the strength to do the right thing even though it may be difficult.

Covet: a strong desire for something that does not belong to you.

Dedication: a virtue that keeps a person attached to a good cause even when it's not easy.

False witness: lying.

Gluttony: eating and drinking too much.

Golden mean: the idea that virtue can be found in the mid-point between extremes.

Golden rule: a guide for relationships with others that Jesus and other religious leaders taught: "In everything do to others as you would have them do to you." (Matthew 7:12)

Habit: an automatic pattern of behaviour, when we do things without thinking about them.

Parable: a story that uses everyday situations to teach deep truths.

Psychologist: a person who studies the human mind, particularly how it affects behaviour.

Sabbath: a day of rest and worship. For almost all Christians, the Sabbath is on Sunday.

Sin: thoughts or actions that harm our relationships, particularly with God.

Sloth: laziness that prevents us from keeping ourselves and our environment clean and tidy.

Theological virtues: faith, hope and love, which are particular gifts from God.

Vice: patterns or habits of bad choices that hurt our friendships with others and with God.

Virtue: an action that reflects God and helps others as well as ourselves.

Wisdom: the virtue of being able to see events clearly and then make good decisions.

Printed on Silva Enviro 100% post-consumer EcoLogo certified paper,
processed chlorine free and manufactured using biogas energy.